SPOTLIGHT ON NATIVE AMERICANS

CHICKASAW

Omar Stone

PowerKiDS
press™

New York

Published in 2016 by The Rosen Publishing Group, Inc.
29 East 21st Street, New York, NY 10010

First Edition

Editor: Sarah Machajewski
Book Design: Samantha DeMartin
Material reviewed by: Donald A. Grinde, Jr., Professor of Transnational/American Studies at the State University of New York at Buffalo.

Photo Credits: Cover, p. 4 David McNew/Getty Images News/Getty Images; p. 7 Peter Hermes Furian/Shutterstock.com; p. 9 (main) UniversalImagesGroup/Universal Images Group/Getty Images; p. 9 (map) Iryna Sunrise/Shutterstock.com; p. 11 19melissa68/Flickr.com; p. 13 courtesy of Library of Congress; pp. 15, 16 danzil raines/Flickr.com; pp. 17, 28–29 Smithsonian's National Museum of the American Indian/Flickr.com; p. 18 Phoebe/Wikimedia Commons; p. 19 MPI/Archive Photos/Getty Images; p. 21 Sheila Brennan/Flickr.com; p. 22 Beinecke Rare Book & Manuscript Library, Yale University/Wikimedia Commons; p. 24 H.L.I.T./Flickr.com; p. 25 (both) Kym Koch Thompson/Wikimedia Commons; p. 27 fine_plan/Flickr.com.

Library of Congress Cataloging-in-Publication Data

Stone, Omar, author.
 Chickasaw / Omar Stone.
     pages cm. — (Spotlight on Native Americans)
 Includes index.
 ISBN 978-1-5081-4105-1 (pbk.)
 ISBN 978-1-5081-4106-8 (6 pack)
 ISBN 978-1-5081-4108-2 (library binding)
 1. Chickasaw Indians—Juvenile literature. 2. Chickasaw Indians—History—Juvenile literature. I. Title.
 E99.C55S76 2016
 976.004'97386—dc23
                              2015034093

Manufactured in the United States of America

CPSIA Compliance Information: Batch #BW16PK: For Further Information contact Rosen Publishing, New York, New York at 1-800-237-9932

CONTENTS

WHO ARE THE CHICKASAWS?

CHAPTER 1

Native American groups occupied lands in North America hundreds of years before Europeans arrived. Their ancestors occupied the same lands thousands of years before that. Today, there are more than 500 Native American groups in the United States. In Canada, there are more than 600 groups.

The history of the Chickasaws dates back thousands of years. Ancestors of the Chickasaws may have lived in what's today the southeastern United States as long as 1,400 years ago. The Chickasaws' **unique** identity is thought to have emerged in the 17th century.

Europeans arrived in the so-called New World in the 1500s. Their arrival brought great change to the native peoples living on the continent. The Chickasaw people faced many challenges to their traditional ways of life. However, they preserved their **culture** by holding on to their traditions and celebrating their past. In the face of great strife, they suffered, but also survived. The Chickasaw people's ability to adapt in a changing world has allowed them to become one of the strongest and most successful Native American groups in the United States.

The Chickasaw people of today have made a great effort to celebrate their past by teaching others about their culture. They often perform traditional dances and ceremonies wearing traditional clothing. Making art using **techniques** from the past is another way they honor their culture.

GREAT MIGRATIONS

CHAPTER 2

The Chickasaws lived in the Southeast long before Europeans arrived in North America. However, their ancestors weren't originally from there. Some people think ancestors of Native Americans may have come from eastern Asia.

According to this theory, Earth experienced an ice age thousands of years ago. An ice age is a period of time marked by very cold temperatures. Sea levels were much lower than they are today because most of the water was frozen in great ice sheets. Because of the low sea levels, places that are covered by water today were once dry. This includes the area between eastern Asia and Alaska. We call the land that connected these landmasses a land bridge. Ancestors of Native Americans may have used this land bridge to **migrate** from Asia to North America.

If this theory is correct, these ancestral migrations would've taken place more than 12,000 years ago, but historians aren't exactly sure. In the thousands of years since then, sea levels rose and covered the land bridge.

As water levels rose, ancestral Native Americans continued their migration, traveling around the continent. Today, a body of water called the Bering Strait separates Asia and North America.

The land bridge that may have been used during these ancient migrations is thought to have been about 600 miles (966 km) wide in some places.

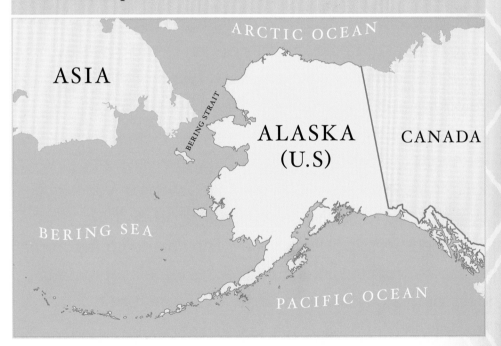

THE ORIGINAL HOMELANDS
CHAPTER 3

Over thousands of years, Earth's climate warmed and became similar to the climate we have today. Ancestors of Native Americans spread out and settled throughout North America and eventually lost contact with each other. The earliest peoples were hunters and gatherers, which means they hunted wild animals and collected plants to survive. Many of these groups eventually began farming, which allowed for permanent settlements. Over time, these groups developed separate cultures and lifestyles that reflected where they lived.

Ancestors of the Chickasaw people were part of the Mound-Builder societies that lived thousands of years ago. They belonged to the Mississippian Mound Builders, who lived in the Mississippi River valley. Their name comes from the large earthen mounds they built near their settlements. Known for being skilled craftsmen and farmers, the Mississippian Mound Builders lasted until around 1500.

The time period beginning around 1500 is known as the historic period. The Chickasaws of this **era** lived in what's today Mississippi, Alabama, Tennessee, and Kentucky.

These areas are considered to be the Chickasaws' homelands. The natural geography of these places included forests, mountains, prairies, and waterways such as the Mississippi River.

places in which the Chickasaws originally lived

UNITED STATES

Kentucky

Tennessee

Mississippi

Alabama

Most mounds were rectangular and had flattened tops. Mounds had different uses. Some were used for burial, while others were the site of temples. Worshipers reached the temple using stairs built into the mound.

THE BIG WHITE DOG AND THE SACRED POLE

CHAPTER 4

Most Native American groups have an origin story that explains how their people came to exist and live on the earth. Each origin story is different. There are often different **versions** of the same story among people of the same community. This is just one version of a Chickasaw origin story.

A long time ago, a group of Indians lived in the West. They were constantly at war with an enemy, but sought peace and comfort. Tired of the constant battling, the people went to wise **prophets** for advice. The prophets thought about it for a long time. They asked their creator god, Ubabeneli, what to do.

The wise prophets told the people they should seek a new home where they could find happiness and peace. They would be guided by a sacred pole, called *kohta falaya*, that had been made by Ubabeneli. After each day of their journey, the people were to stick *kohta falaya* in the ground. Whichever way it leaned was the direction they had to travel. When the pole stood upright, they would have their new home. On the first day of their journey, *kohta falaya* pointed east.

kohta falaya

This origin story explains how important animals and natural forces were to the way Chickasaw society developed.

To make the journey easier, the people split into two groups. A young chief called Chickasaw led one group. His brother, a chief called Choctaw, led the other group. The groups set out on their long journey, which took them in the direction of the sunrise.

The migrating people didn't take this journey alone. A white dog walked in front of them. It was their guard and scout. The dog also let the people know if enemies were nearby. If anyone in the group became sick, the white dog helped them feel better. The people loved the dog very much.

Every morning, the *kohta falaya* pointed east. The journey was long and slow, and they passed through other Native Americans' lands. One night, the people reached the Mississippi River. They rafted across, but unfortunately, the white dog was swept downstream.

The people rested for many days after crossing the river. One morning, they woke up and the *kohta falaya* was wobbling and pointing in many directions. The brothers, Chickasaw and Choctaw, couldn't agree about what to do next. Chief Choctaw felt their home had been reached. Chief Chickasaw felt the people had to continue their journey east. He commanded those who believed him to follow him, and they did. One hundred miles (161 km) later, the sacred pole stood upright, and the Chickasaw people had reached their home.

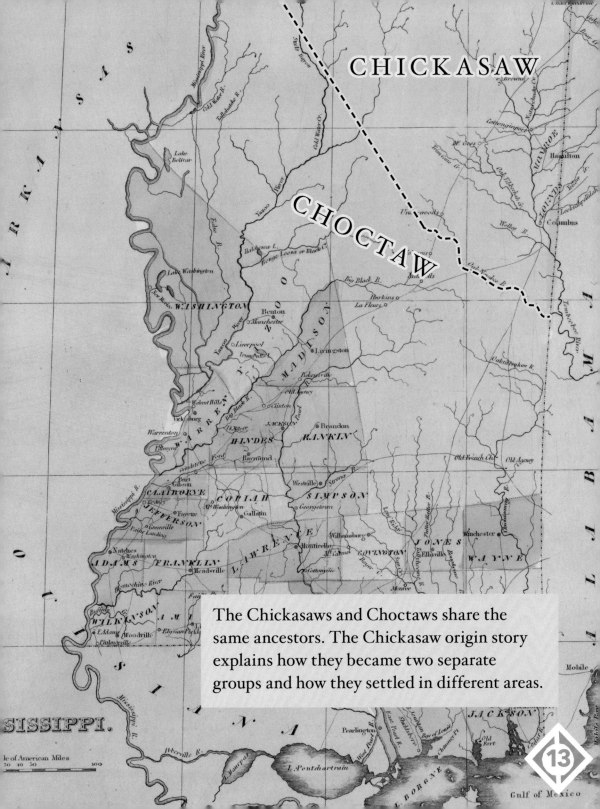

The Chickasaws and Choctaws share the same ancestors. The Chickasaw origin story explains how they became two separate groups and how they settled in different areas.

CHICKASAW SOCIETY
CHAPTER 5

Once the Chickasaws settled in their homelands, they developed a unique culture and identity. In 1650, their population was between 15,000 and 20,000, making them the largest of the three native communities that lived in Mississippi. The Chickasaws often traded food and supplies with the Choctaws, who were accomplished farmers. The Chickasaws themselves were known for their skilled hunting abilities.

Traditionally, Chickasaws lived in villages and towns. The biggest towns probably had about 200 households. Each household had a winter house, a summer house, a building for holding corn, and other buildings. Each village had a long fort, an area where ceremonies were performed, and a house where councils met. Villages had ball courts where stickball, a popular sport, was played. A tall fence made of logs surrounded each village and provided protection.

The Chickasaw people were organized into **clans**. People belonged to their mother's clan. Each clan was different and had an animal that represented what the clan stood for. The Iksa' Shawi' (Raccoon Clan), Iksa' Kowishto' Losa' (Panther Clan), and Iksa' Kowimilhlha' (Wildcat Clan) are just some examples. Clans were the most important group people belonged to. The fact that they were named after animals also shows how important animals were to Chickasaw society.

This is an example of what a Chickasaw village and its buildings might have looked like.

CHICKASAW MEN AND WOMEN

CHAPTER 6

Chickasaw men and women had different **roles** in society. Men were hunters and warriors. Many men also became great storytellers, artists, and **medicine men**. Chickasaw women performed tasks that kept them closer to the home. Though the

Chickasaws weren't a farming society, they still grew crops. Women were in charge of growing crops such as beans, corn, and squash, which are known as the three sisters. Women also raised children. Chickasaw women could be great storytellers and artists. In the past, only men could become chiefs.

Traditionally, Chickasaws made their clothes from materials found in nature, including plants and animal skins.

During summer, men wore a **breechcloth** and deerskin shirt, as well as moccasins. During the winter, they wore leggings, a shirt, and boots made of animal skin. Chickasaw men shaved the sides of their head, leaving just one long strip of hair in the middle of their head. They painted their faces to show what clan they belonged to. Warriors wore eagle and swan feathers, which were a great honor. Women wore animal-skin dresses and sometimes added shells or beads for decoration. They wore conch shells as earrings and spent much time caring for their hair, which they often wore pulled back.

Chickasaw clothing changed greatly after Europeans arrived. Both men and women began wearing European-style clothes.

CHANGE COMES TO THE CHICKASAWS

CHAPTER 7

The Chickasaws' traditional ways of life were mostly undisturbed until the 1500s, when Europeans arrived in North America. The Chickasaws' first encounter with Europeans was when Hernando de Soto, who was a Spanish explorer, arrived in what's today the southeastern United States in 1540. He and a crew of men traveled through Chickasaw homelands, but didn't stay there long.

That marked the beginning of European colonization of North America. Over the next 200 years, the Spanish, French, and British settled in Chickasaw territory. The Chickasaws started trading with the British in the late 1600s, after Britain founded the Carolina colonies. Chickasaws now had

European-style tools and guns, which allowed them to become powerful. They used their weapons to raid nearby Choctaw communities.

The Chickasaws continued to trade with Europeans as more arrived in the so-called New World. These relationships eventually carried over into war. Known for being successful and fierce warriors, many Chickasaw men joined in the fighting during the **French and Indian War**. They fought with the British against the French, who had been joined by other Native American groups. Many Chickasaws also fought with colonists during the American Revolution. Though the Chickasaws supported the new United States, they quickly learned the United States wouldn't be so kind to them.

After Europeans arrived in North America, the Chickasaws' traditional ways of life changed. They traded for European-style tools, began using guns, and started wearing clothes like the white settlers wore.

THE GREAT REMOVAL
CHAPTER 8

Throughout the 18th and 19th centuries, the U.S. government passed laws that **discriminated** against Native Americans. Many of these policies forced Native Americans to give up their culture and their land.

In 1786, the Chickasaws signed the Treaty of Hopewell. Chief Piominko signed on behalf of the Chickasaws. The treaty established boundaries on Chickasaw land and gave the Chickasaws the right to protect it. While the treaty may have seemed good at first, the U.S. government later used it against the Chickasaws to take more land and further limit their rights.

In the 1820s and 1830s, the U.S. government wanted to own land in the southeastern United States that belonged to the Chickasaws and other Native American groups. The government passed the Indian Removal Act to force the Chickasaws and other native people off it.

The government forced many Native American groups to accept land west of the Mississippi River in exchange for their land in the East. However, the Chickasaws wanted money. In 1836, the U.S. government agreed to pay them $3 million for their land. In 1837, the Chickasaws relocated. Known as the "Great Removal," Chickasaw families walked hundreds of miles to land in Oklahoma with little food and without proper clothing. It was a time of terrible sorrow and suffering.

one trail used during the Great Removal

The Chickasaws were the last group to leave the Southeast under the Indian Removal Act. Today, the Chickasaw Nation says its ancestors may have suffered less than other groups because they were able to relocate on their own terms. For example, they chose to leave during favorable weather conditions, which probably saved lives.

MOVING TO INDIAN TERRITORY

CHAPTER 9

The Chickasaws relocated to Indian Territory in present-day Oklahoma in 1837. They signed the Treaty of Doaksville with the Choctaws, who allowed Chickasaws to purchase land on their new territory for $530,000. Then, the Chickasaws left their homelands in three groups. By the end of the forced removal, about 4,000 Chickasaws had relocated.

The Chickasaws lived on Choctaw territory for more than 10 years. In that time, the Chickasaws focused on creating their own educational system and their own economy. The Chickasaws founded

schools, or *holissaapisas*, in the 1840s and boarding schools in the 1850s. Many Chickasaw families formed ranches and plantations and sold their products, which allowed them to earn their own money. They ultimately desired to be a **sovereign** nation once again and worked to separate from the Choctaws.

In 1855, it happened. The groups signed a treaty of separation. In 1856, the Chickasaw Nation formed. Its capital was in Tishomingo, Oklahoma. The new government was split into branches, much like the U.S. government. Cyrus Harris was elected the first governor of the Chickasaw Nation. Under his leadership, the Chickasaws worked toward becoming a strong and successful nation once again.

Many Native American children were forced to attend boarding schools. They weren't allowed to practice their traditional **customs** or speak their native language. The Native American children in this picture are wearing European-style clothing, which was also a practice enforced in boarding schools. The most well-known Chickasaw boarding school was Bloomfield Academy. It remained open until 1949.

A NEW NATION EMERGES

CHAPTER 10

While the Chickasaws worked to rebuild their nation, the U.S. government continued to make decisions that affected them. In 1907, Oklahoma became a state, and the Chickasaws then became citizens of Oklahoma. In 1924, the Indian Citizenship Act granted all native people, including Chickasaws, full U.S. citizenship. The Chickasaws supported Congress's Indian Reorganization Act of 1934, which was meant to protect Native Americans' lands and rights. Over the next few decades, Chickasaws worked tirelessly to be seen as equal in the eyes of the U.S. government.

In 1972, the Chickasaw Nation bought its first business. The Chickasaw Motor Inn earned $100,000 in its first year. It was just the beginning of an economic and cultural **renaissance** for the Chickasaw people. Over the years, the Chickasaws have worked to start businesses, which give jobs to tribal members. This includes Chickasaw Nation Industries, Bedré Chocolates, Bank2, and WinStar **Casinos**. These businesses employ thousands of people in multiple states.

The nation has also launched cultural, economic, and educational programs for its people, which work to preserve the Chickasaws' past and celebrate their present and promising future. The Chickasaw Historical Society, Chickasaw Cultural Center, and Chickasaw Press work together to teach people about the Chickasaws' important identity.

The Chickasaw Nation was once one of the poorest Native American groups in the United States. Through hard work and determination, the Chickasaws have become one of the most successful tribal groups today. The Chickasaw Nation works to put money into cultural programs, resources, and financial assistance for its members.

KEEPING CULTURE ALIVE

CHAPTER 11

Today, there are around 60,000 people in the United States who have Chickasaw citizenship. To belong to the Chickasaw Nation, members must prove they have at least one Chickasaw ancestor. Today's Chickasaws come from all walks of life and live around the world. Chickasaws have become congressmen, doctors, lawyers, and other important figures in their communities. John Herrington, a Chickasaw citizen and also an astronaut, holds the honor of being the first Native American in space. In 2002, Herrington carried a flag of the Chickasaw Nation and an eagle feather with him on his 13-day mission into space.

Many Chickasaws work hard to keep Chickasaw culture alive. These Culture Keepers preserve the traditions through storytelling, dance, drumming, and art. Many Chickasaws create art such as traditional costumes and clothing, pottery, tools, and musical instruments. They use techniques that have been passed down through generations, which is something that helps them feel closer to their past.

Both Chickasaw citizens as well as nonnatives can visit the cultural centers and historic sites in Alabama, Florida, Kentucky, Illinois, Mississippi, Oklahoma, and Tennessee to explore the journey of the Chickasaw people.

These men and women, who were photographed in 2014, practice a traditional Chickasaw dance.

A GREAT NATION

CHAPTER 12

The story of the Chickasaw people dates back thousands of years. Their ancestors may have crossed a land bridge into North America. They then became part of a culture of Mound Builders who settled in the Southeast and began farming. From that culture, a society of warriors and expert hunters grew to become a powerful force in the precolonial era. After the arrival of Europeans, the Chickasaws held fast to their traditions while also adapting in some ways to the changes that surrounded them. When the Chickasaws were forcibly removed from their land, they organized and worked to become strong and powerful. Today, the Chickasaw Nation is very successful and has adapted, once again, to a modern and changing world.

Through every part of the Chickasaws' history, the people have worked to maintain their identity in the face of great change. Their efforts to preserve and celebrate their past have created a powerful legacy. While they no longer live as their ancestors once did, today's Chickasaws still embody the same courage and determination of spirit.

At the Chikasha Poya—We Are Chickasaw festival—visitors learn about Chickasaw culture through hands-on arts and crafts activities, storytelling, live music, traditional dances, and artist booths. Chickasaws from around the country participate in this festival every year.

GLOSSARY

breechcloth: A piece of clothing worn around the waist.

casino: A public place where gambling games take place.

clan: An extended family.

culture: The beliefs and ways of life of a group of people.

custom: A traditional way of doing something.

discriminate: To treat unequally.

era: A long period of time with a particular feature or characteristic.

French and Indian War: From 1754 to 1763, a war between the British and French over territory in North America.

medicine man: A person believed to have healing powers.

migrate: To move from one area to another.

prophet: A person who claims to be able to communicate with or receive messages from their gods.

renaissance: A revival or new interest in something.

role: A part someone has in a particular situation.

sovereign: Independent.

technique: A way of doing something.

unique: Special or different.

version: A form of something that is slightly different from other forms of the same type of thing.

FOR MORE INFORMATION

BOOKS

Barnes, Wiley. *C Is for Chickasaw*. Ada, OK: White Dog Press, 2014.

Chickasaw Press. *Chickasaw Journeys Activity Book*. Ada, OK: White Dog Press, 2014.

Gray-Kanatiiosh, Barbara A. *Chickasaw*. Edina, MN: ABDO Publishing, 2007.

WEBSITES

Due to the changing nature of Internet links, PowerKids Press has developed an online list of websites related to the subject of this book. This site is updated regularly. Please use this link to access the list: www.powerkidslinks.com/sona/chck

INDEX